Endangered Butterflies

Bobbie Kalman & Robin Johnson

🌳 Crabtree Publishing Company

www.crabtreebooks.com

Earth's Endangered Animals Series
A Bobbie Kalman Book

Dedicated by Robin Johnson
For Tony, who still gives me butterflies

Editor-in-Chief
Bobbie Kalman

Writing team
Bobbie Kalman
Robin Johnson

Substantive editor
Kathryn Smithyman

Editors
Molly Aloian
Kelley MacAulay

Design
Katherine Kantor

Production coordinator
Heather Fitzpatrick

Photo research
Crystal Foxton

Consultant
Patricia Loesche, Ph.D., Animal Behavior Program,
Department of Psychology, University of Washington

Illustrations
Bonna Rouse: back cover, pages 4, 10 (middle left swallowtail), 11, 12, 14, 29
Margaret Amy Salter: pages 10 (except middle left swallowtail), 24, 31

Photographs
Animals Animals - Earth Scenes: © Degginger, E.R.: page 29;
   © Nicolini, Stefano: page 25
© Pavel Losevsky. Image from BigStockPhoto.com: page 21
Bruce Coleman Inc.: G.E. Hyde: page 27
Pat Canova/Index Stock: page 9
iStockphoto.com: Diane Diederich: page 8; Wesley Jarmusch: page 31;
   Daniel Thomas: page 23 (top)
Ernie Janes/NHPA: page 16
Photo Researchers, Inc.: Ron Austing: page 17; Dr. John Brackenbury: page 26
Michael P. Turco: page 28
Visuals Unlimited: Wally Eberhart: page 20; Ross Frid: page 18
Other images by Brand X Pictures, Corel, Creatas, and Digital Stock

Crabtree Publishing Company

www.crabtreebooks.com   1-800-387-7650

Cataloging-in-Publication Data
Kalman, Bobbie.
   Endangered butterflies / Bobbie Kalman & Robin Johnson.
     p. cm. -- (Earth's endangered animals)
   Includes index.
   ISBN-13: 978-0-7787-1870-3 (rlb)
   ISBN-10: 0-7787-1870-0 (rlb)
   ISBN-13: 978-0-7787-1916-8 (pbk)
   ISBN-10: 0-7787-1916-2 (pbk)
   1. Butterflies--Juvenile literature. 2. Endangered species--
Juvenile literature. I. Johnson, Robin (Robin R.) II. Title.
   QL544.2.K3515 2006
   595.78'9--dc22
                                            2005036719
                                                LC

**Published in
the United States**
PMB 16A
350 Fifth Ave.
Suite 3308
New York, NY
10118

**Published
in Canada**
616 Welland Ave.
St. Catharines, Ontario
L2M 5V6

**Published in the
United Kingdom**
White Cross Mills
High Town, Lancaster
LA1 4XS

**Published
in Australia**
386 Mt. Alexander Rd.
Ascot Vale (Melbourne)
VIC 3032

Contents

Endangered butterflies

There are more than 15,000 **species**, or types, of butterflies in the world! Many butterfly species are **endangered**. Some species of butterflies have already become **extinct**.

Danger ahead

There are thousands of butterfly species, so it is difficult for scientists to know when a species becomes endangered. Some butterflies are known to be endangered, but many more face problems that could soon cause them to become endangered. For example, many butterflies are losing the plants on which they feed or lay their eggs. Keep reading to find out why butterflies need our help to stay alive!

The Xerces Blue butterfly is an extinct butterfly species.

4

Words to know

Scientists use certain words to describe animals in danger. Some of these words are listed here.

vulnerable Describes animals that may soon become endangered

endangered Describes animals that are in danger of dying out in the **wild**, or natural areas not controlled by people

critically endangered Describes animals that are at high risk of dying out in the wild

extinct Describes animals that have died out in the wild or animals that have not been seen in the wild for at least 50 years

This Regal Fritillary is an endangered butterfly.

What are butterflies?

There are more than one million kinds of insects in the world! This pipevine swallowtail is an insect.

Butterflies are **insects**. Insects are **cold-blooded** animals. The body temperatures of cold-blooded animals change when the temperatures of their surroundings change. Insects are **invertebrates**, or animals that do not have **backbones**. Instead of backbones, insects have hard coverings on the outside of their bodies. These protective coverings are called **exoskeletons**.

Insect bodies

An insect's body is divided into three parts—a head, a **thorax**, and an **abdomen**. An insect has two **antennae** on its head. It has six legs on its thorax. Many insects, including butterflies, also have wings attached to their thoraxes.

Scale wings

Butterflies belong to an **order**, or group, of insects called *Lepidoptera*. Lepidoptera means "scale wing." Butterflies have two pairs of large, colorful wings that are covered with tiny scales.

Moths also have wings with scales and belong to the same insect group as butterflies. Moths are different from butterflies, however. Some of the differences between moths and butterflies are listed below.

Butterflies

- often have brightly colored wings
- have antennae that are long and thin, with tiny knobs on the ends
- have slender, hairless bodies
- are usually active during the day
- rest with their wings straight up in the air

Moths

- often have dull-colored wings
- have antennae that are different shapes and sizes
- have thick, furry bodies
- are usually active at night
- rest with their wings folded over their bodies

Butterflies everywhere!

Butterflies live all over the world. They are found on every **continent** except Antarctica. Different butterflies live in different **habitats**.

A habitat is the natural place where an animal lives. Butterflies live in meadows, in forests, in deserts, and on mountains.

These butterflies are visiting a field of daisies in their meadow habitat.

Rainforest habitats

Most butterfly species live in **rain forests**. A rain forest is a hot, thick forest that receives over 80 inches (203 cm) of rain each year. Birdwing butterflies and other butterflies that live in rain forests need the hot, wet **climate** in order to survive.

The life cycle of a butterfly

Every animal goes through a set of changes as it grows. This set of changes is called a **life cycle**. A butterfly's life cycle begins inside an egg. The insect grows and changes until it is **mature**, or an adult. A mature butterfly can **mate**, or join together with another butterfly to make babies. After mating, female butterflies lay eggs. A new life cycle begins with each egg.

This leafwing butterfly is an adult.

Time flies for butterflies

Most butterflies have short **life spans**. A life span is the length of time an animal is alive. Most species of butterflies live only for a few weeks. Some species of butterflies live for several months, however.

Complete metamorphosis

The set of changes a butterfly goes through during its life cycle is called **complete metamorphosis**. A butterfly's metamorphosis is made up of four stages—egg, **larva**, **pupa**, and adult.

A butterfly life cycle begins in an egg.

*A larva hatches from the egg. The larva is called a **caterpillar**. The caterpillar eats and grows.*

The insect that comes out of the chrysalis is an adult butterfly. Its metamorphosis is complete.

*The caterpillar makes a case called a **chrysalis** around itself. When it is inside its chrysalis, the insect is called a pupa. The pupa's body turns to liquid and then begins to develop adult body parts.*

11

Built for eating

Caterpillars spend a lot of time eating! They eat mainly plant parts, such as leaves and stems. Some also eat flowers, fruit, vegetables, wood, and other insects. Caterpillars have bodies that are built for eating.

They have strong jaws and teeth for chewing. They have six legs, called **true legs**, which they use for gripping plants. Most caterpillars also have ten **prolegs**. They use their prolegs to walk.

A caterpillar's prolegs have tiny hooks on them for clinging to plants.

A caterpillar has poor eyesight. It can sense only light and darkness.

*A caterpillar **digests**, or breaks down, its food inside its abdomen.*

A caterpillar's true legs are attached to its thorax. These six legs will become the butterfly's legs.

*A caterpillar's **mouthparts** are large and strong.*

Good hosts

Although they have big appetites, many caterpillars eat only certain plants, called **host plants**. Host plants are the plants on which some species of butterflies lay their eggs. When caterpillars hatch from the eggs, they eat the host plants.

Monarchs and milkweed

A female monarch butterfly lays her eggs only on a host plant called milkweed. When monarch caterpillars hatch from the eggs, they feed on the milkweed plants. Without milkweed, monarch caterpillars cannot survive.

This hungry monarch caterpillar is chewing its way through a milkweed plant.

13

Built for flying

Butterflies are built for flying. They have light bodies and strong wings. They use their wings to fly from flower to flower, searching for food. Unlike a caterpillar, a butterfly does not have mouthparts for chewing leaves. Instead, a butterfly has a long tongue called a **proboscis**. The butterfly uses its proboscis like a straw to drink **nectar**. Nectar is a sweet liquid found in some flowers. Some butterflies also drink juice from rotting fruit, sap from trees, or dew from grass.

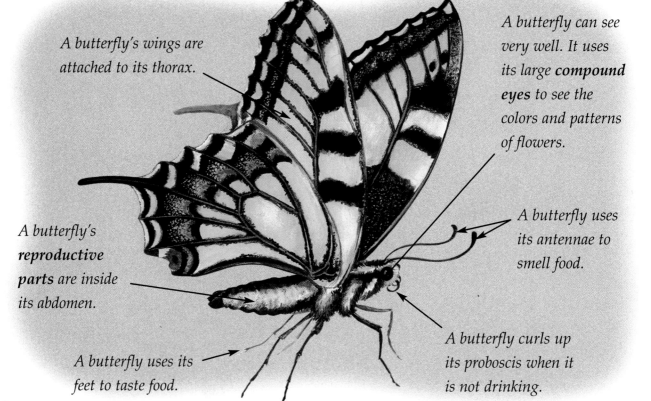

A butterfly's wings are attached to its thorax.

*A butterfly can see very well. It uses its large **compound eyes** to see the colors and patterns of flowers.*

*A butterfly's **reproductive parts** are inside its abdomen.*

A butterfly uses its antennae to smell food.

A butterfly uses its feet to taste food.

A butterfly curls up its proboscis when it is not drinking.

Pollen movers

Butterflies are **pollinators**, or animals that help spread **pollen** from plant to plant. Pollen is a powdery substance found in flowers. Flowers need pollen from other flowers to make seeds. As a butterfly drinks nectar from a flower, pollen from the flower often sticks to the butterfly's body. When the butterfly flies to another flower to drink nectar, it carries the pollen with it on its body. Some of the pollen may rub off on that flower.

This heliconius butterfly has yellow pollen on its body.

Surviving the cold

This Brimstone butterfly is hibernating in some ivy.

Some butterfly species live in habitats that have cold winters. Many of these species lay their eggs and then die when winter weather arrives. A few butterfly species **hibernate** to survive the cold weather.

Hibernation

Butterflies that hibernate survive winter by entering **dormant**, or sleeplike, states. Butterflies may hibernate when they are eggs, larvae, pupae, or adults. They spend winter in sheltered spots, where they are protected from the weather and from **predators**. Hibernating butterflies may live under leaves, in caves, or even in people's homes!

Migrating butterflies

Some butterfly species **migrate** to avoid cold weather, which would kill them. To migrate means to move to a new place to live for a certain period of time. Other butterfly species migrate to avoid hot or dry weather, to find food, or to find host plants on which to lay their eggs.

One-way trips

Monarch butterflies are one of the few species of migrating butterflies that return to their former homes. Most species of migrating butterflies move from place to place in search of food, host plants, and the climates they need to survive.

Habitat loss

One of the biggest threats to butterflies is **habitat loss**. Habitat loss is the destruction of the natural places where animals live. People destroy butterfly habitats by **logging**, or cutting down trees and selling the wood. People also destroy butterfly habitats by **clearing** fields to make roads and build houses. Clearing is removing all the plants from an area.

Homeless butterflies

When the plants in their habitats are destroyed, butterflies have nowhere to live or to lay their eggs. They also have no food to eat.

The endangered Karner Blue butterfly lays its eggs only on wild lupine plants. After hatching, Karner Blue caterpillars feed only on the wild lupines. Unfortunately, people are destroying many of these plants.

Rain forests in danger

Rain forests around the world are being destroyed at an alarming rate! People destroy about 54,000 square miles (140,000 km²) of rain forest each year. Many butterflies that live in rain forests are endangered because people are destroying their habitats. In fact, some species of rainforest butterflies may become extinct even before they are discovered by people.

This Rajah Brooke's Birdwing butterfly lives in a rain forest in Malaysia. It is endangered.

19

Chemical dangers

As pollinators, butterflies are helpful to people and other living things. Many people believe that caterpillars are pests, however. Caterpillars eat the plants in gardens and the **crops** in fields. Crops are plants grown by people for food. For this reason, some people kill caterpillars with **pesticides**. Pesticides are chemicals that farmers and gardeners spray on plants to kill insects.

Some people believe that cabbage white caterpillars are pests. These insects can destroy entire crops of cabbage, broccoli, and other vegetables.

20

Herbicides

Some people use chemicals called **herbicides** on their fields and gardens. Herbicides kill the weeds and wild plants on which they are sprayed. Unfortunately, some of the weeds and wild plants that people kill are the host plants that caterpillars and butterflies need in order to survive.

Butterfly populations

Without their host plants, some butterflies have nowhere to lay their eggs. If butterflies do not lay eggs, they cannot increase their **population**. Population is the total number of one species living in an area. If certain butterfly populations **decline**, or drop, those butterflies may become endangered or extinct.

21

Collecting butterflies

Some people collect butterflies and other insects and display them in cases, as shown below. Butterfly hunters are people who capture and kill butterflies and then sell them to butterfly collectors. The collectors value butterflies for their delicate bodies and beautiful wings. Unfortunately, many collectors want rainforest butterflies or other butterflies that are already endangered. When people collect endangered butterflies, these butterfly species are at greater risk of becoming extinct.

Some rare species of butterflies sell for hundreds or even thousands of dollars!

Butterfly hunters travel to rain forests to kill millions of Blue Morpho butterflies. Collectors and jewelry makers value the Blue Morpho for its shimmering blue wings.

Butterfly boutique

Some people use butterflies to make jewelry such as necklaces, pins, and earrings. To make jewelry, colorful butterfly wings are clipped and sometimes painted. The wings are then put in glass or plastic and mounted on the jewelry.

Butterfly ranches

Some jewelry makers and collectors buy butterflies from **butterfly ranches**. A butterfly ranch is a place where people raise butterflies in order to sell them.

More about monarchs

Each fall, millions of monarch butterflies migrate to Mexico from eastern Canada and the United States. The monarchs travel as far as 2,800 miles (4506 km) to spend winter in **Oyamel fir forests**.

Oyamel fir forests are dense forests found only on mountains in Mexico. These forests have the right climate for monarchs. The thick, tall trees also protect the monarchs from rain and wind.

Danger in winter

Today there is more logging of Oyamel fir trees than there was in the past. These forests are now smaller and have fewer trees. When there are fewer trees, monarch butterflies have fewer places to live in their winter habitats.

Danger in summer

When monarchs return to their summer habitats, they face other dangers. People often destroy the milkweed plants on which monarchs lay their eggs because people consider milkweed plants to be weeds. Without host plants in summer and without places to live in winter, monarchs may soon have nowhere at all to live!

If logging in Mexico continues at the present rate, all the Oyamel fir trees will be gone by the year 2050. Millions of monarch butterflies will have nowhere to land!

Protecting butterflies

People around the world are working to protect butterflies in the wild. Governments in many countries have passed **conservation laws**. These laws ban people from harming endangered butterflies.

Trading block

Many species of endangered butterflies are also protected by **CITES**. CITES is a document signed by the governments of 169 countries around the world. The governments of these countries have made it against the law to **trade**, or buy and sell, rare species of animals. By preventing the trade of rare species, CITES helps stop people from killing and collecting endangered butterflies.

The endangered Apollo butterfly is protected by conservation laws in many countries in Europe. CITES also forbids people to buy or sell this butterfly.

Reserves

Although laws and trade agreements help protect butterflies from collectors, they do not protect butterflies from their greatest threat—the loss of their habitats. In order to protect endangered butterflies and their homes, some countries have turned butterfly habitats into **reserves**. Reserves are areas of land that governments purchase. They then protect these areas from being damaged or **developed**. Reserves are patrolled by **rangers**. Rangers are people who make sure that the butterflies and other animals on the reserves are kept safe.

*Large copper butterflies became extinct in Britain in 1851, when their habitat was destroyed. A rare **subspecies** of this butterfly, shown above, is now found only on a reserve in the Netherlands. Conservation laws protect this butterfly.*

People helping butterflies

Although governments and people try to protect butterflies, the populations of many species are now dangerously low. To help these species survive, researchers around the world are studying endangered butterflies. By studying the butterflies, researchers learn what they need in order to survive. They also learn how to protect the butterflies from becoming extinct.

This researcher is netting an endangered Schaus' Swallowtail butterfly. He will study the butterfly and then release it unharmed.

Breeding butterflies

In order to increase the populations of endangered butterflies, scientists **breed** some species of butterflies. To breed means to allow animals of the same species to mate and have babies in **captivity**. Some butterflies remain in captivity after people breed them. People take other butterflies to preserves or release them into the wild.

This endangered birdwing butterfly was raised by researchers. It has just emerged from its chrysalis.

The Xerces Society was named after the Xerces Blue butterfly, which is now extinct.

The Xerces Society

The Xerces Society is a conservation group that is dedicated to protecting butterflies and other invertebrates. The Xerces Society works with researchers, schools, governments, and concerned citizens, to teach people how to **conserve**, or save, butterflies and their habitats.

You can help, too!

Butterflies are attracted to red, orange, yellow, purple, and dark-pink flowers. These Eastern Tiger Swallowtails are resting on some pink flowers.

You can help butterflies where you live by planting a butterfly-friendly garden. Begin by choosing a variety of brightly colored flowering plants that are **native** to your area. The colors and smells of the plants will attract different butterflies to your garden. If there are certain butterflies you would like to attract, be sure to include their favorite flowers and their host plants in your garden.

Welcome, butterflies!

To grow, most plants need a lot of sunlight, so make sure you choose a sunny spot for your plants. Butterflies will visit your garden to rest, warm their wings in the sun, and sip nectar from your flowers.

More ways to help

There are many other ways that you can help save butterflies in your neighborhood.

• Ask your friends never to collect butterflies or even to touch them. Touching butterflies can cause the scales on the wings of the butterflies to rub off. Butterflies cannot fly with damaged wings.

• If your parents use harmful chemicals on their lawns and gardens, encourage them to stop. The chemicals kill many caterpillars and butterflies.

• Clean up litter in the fields, forests, and other wild places in your neighborhood. Keep butterfly habitats clean!

• Build or purchase a **butterfly house**. Butterfly houses provide butterflies with safe places to rest. Some butterflies also hibernate in the houses.

Butterfly "Net"

To find out more about butterflies, visit your local library or go online. Here are a few good butterfly websites to get you started:

• **www.xerces.org**
At this informative website, you can read about the efforts of an insect conservation group.

• **www.enchantedlearning.com/ subjects/butterfly/**
This educational website has a butterfly dictionary, activities, and a lot of fun things to print out.

• **www.billybear4kids.com/butterfly/ flutter-fun.html**
Visit this fun website to play butterfly games, make crafts, and send e-cards to your friends.

Glossary

Note: Boldfaced words that are defined in the text may not appear in the glossary.

abdomen The rear section of a butterfly's body

antennae A pair of feelers that certain animals use to sense motion and scent

backbone A row of bones in the middle of an animal's back

captivity A state of living in an enclosed area such as a zoo

chrysalis A hard case that a caterpillar makes around itsef to become a pupa

climate The normal weather conditions in an area

compound eye An eye that is made up of thousands of tiny parts

continent One of the seven large areas of land on Earth—Africa, Antarctica, Asia, Australia, Europe, North America, and South America

crops Plants grown by people for food

develop To construct buildings or make roads in an area

native Describing an animal or plant that is from a particular place or area

predator An animal that hunts and eats other animals

reproductive parts The body parts an animal uses to make babies

subspecies A small group of a species

thorax The middle part of a butterfly's body to which legs and wings are attached

Index

1 2 3 4 5 6 7 8 9 0 Printed in the U.S.A. 5 4 3 2 1 0 9 8 7 6